freedom
and resolve

freedom and resolve

FINDING YOUR TRUE HOME IN THE UNIVERSE

by Gangaji

HAMPTON ROADS

Cover photo of Gangaji by Dan Baumbach
Interior designed by Deborah Dutton

Hampton Roads Publishing Company, Inc.
Charlottesville, VA 22906
Distributed by Red Wheel/Weiser, LLC
www.redwheelweiser.com

Sign up for our newsletter and special offers by going to
www.redwheelweiser.com/newsletter/.

ISBN: **978-1-57174-721-1**

Library of Congress Cataloging-in-Publication Data available upon request.

Printed in the United States of America.
EBM
10 9 8 7 6 5 4 3 2 1

contents

*Someone asked Papaji if he was still vigilant,
and he said, "Until my last breath."*

the choice
is yours

After aeons of choosing to tell a story of separation from God, the story seems choiceless. It seems choiceless, but it is not. You have simply been continuing to choose the story that was passed on to you by your ancestors, by your past lives, by your past mistakes, by your past desires. What is choiceless is the truth of who you are.

Choice lies in the mind's ability to either deny that truth or to embrace it. That choice is free will—the freedom of choice. You have no free will regarding who you are. You are that fully and completely. But you do have free will regarding the powers of mind and imagination. You can play as if you are not who you are. You can play as if you almost are, but still not quite. You can play any number of variations and permutations of choosing or denying who you are.

You have played like this for aeons. Eventually, a weariness arises in the play because the play is limited. For all of its display, for all of its beauty, for all of its pain, the play is limited because it is based on the assumption that you are somehow separate from truth, from understanding, from love, from God. The whole play is based on the assumption of separation, and the assumption hardly ever gets investigated. The assumption is believed to be real, and from this belief the play gets very complicated.

I am inviting you to see *who* is really playing.

Taking for granted the truth that you are consciousness, that you are one with God, that you *are* truth, then this taking for granted is a kind of trance or sleep state, where you will one

You are naturally consciousness. What we name *God* is supreme consciousness. You are naturally one with God. You are naturally truth. All the rest is unnatural. It may be normal, but it is not natural. It may be usual, but it is not natural. The play even has its purpose because with the belief in the play and the unnatural normality of it, there is an opportunity to imagine yourself as lost, to experience the pain and the suffering of being lost, of being cast out, of being separate from God. Then this imagination, this play with all of its pain, can give rise to the yearning for reunion of truth in all of its glory.

day imagine that you are separate, that you are lost, and then the search begins again.

In the invitation that is extended from Ramana, the invitation of direct self-inquiry, you have the opportunity to turn your attention to *who* is lost, *who* is separate. You will find no one. There is no one lost. The lost one was fabricated in the mind to begin the play. If your resolve is to investigate intensely, freshly, completely, to not fall asleep by continuing to practice the belief based on the assumption of separation, then you will meet yourself as that very consciousness in which player, seeker, separation, and union appear and disappear.

vigilance:
a call to deeper surrender

Many lucky, graced people have had a taste or a glimpse of what is immortal, of what is the eternal Self. From that taste the question arises, *What next?* or *What should I do now? What do I do with this? Where do I take it?* These questions indicate that more surrender is being called for. There is always an invitation to more deeply surrender. This surrender is vigilance.

Vigilance is often misunderstood. Usually, what passes for vigilance is careful monitoring by the super ego. I'm sure you're very aware of this kind of monitoring: *Oh, I shouldn't have said it that way. I shouldn't have done it that way. I shouldn't have thought that. I should have surrendered.* This monitoring is not vigilance. It is an imitation of vigilance. Vigilance comes from the word *vigil*, meaning to keep vigil. Keeping vigil is a form of worship. Vigilance is a sacred, quiet, peaceful vigil at the flame of truth.

By assuming that the perception of separation from truth is likely, or at least possible, you have the opportunity to keep vigil at the flame of truth. If you are truly vigilant, you will discover yourself as not separate from truth. What's next from that? Deeper vigilance. Deeper discovery. There is no end to true discovery. What can end is your preoccupation with who you thought you were. Your preoccupation with your body, your thoughts, and your emotions can finally end. In fact, the preoccupation continues only as you continue to feed it.

Feed your body. Feeding your body is not a big deal. But feeding your thoughts is a big deal.

Keep the vigil as long as there is any possibility of a perception of someone separate from truth, as long as there is still a winding down of past desires, as long as there is any breath left in the body.

Feeding your emotions is a big deal. Stop feeding your thoughts and your emotions and see what doesn't need feeding for its existence. Keep vigil by that, surrender to that.

If the arrow of truth has pierced you and you know it, if you have had this experience, then you also know the arrogant thoughts that can arise: *Well, I know I'm one with Truth, so who is there to keep vigil?* You have probably said this, right? Then all of a sudden, there is suffering again with the wailing, *I've lost it! How did this happen?* The perception and experience of losing what cannot be lost are corrected by vigilance.

I am not speaking of effort. I am not speaking of *doing* vigilance. I am speaking of *being* vigilance and recognizing that it is natural to be that. You are pure awareness. Awareness is naturally vigilant. It is vigilant to itself, and it is always, in truth, aware of itself.

When the body is in deep sleep, and there are no reference points, no sense impressions—

no perception of body or any object whether mental, emotional, or physical—still there is awareness aware of itself, and this is bliss. This is the bliss of deep sleep. When the body awakens and objects come back into view, still you know that there has been deep, objectless experience. You don't have any sense impressions of it, but you know it because the awareness of itself is still present. As objects appear, our conditioning is to fixate on the objects and to overlook the deep nourishment that is always present. Vigilance is awareness of what does not disappear even when objects appear. Whether those objects are exquisite or horrible or mundane, always there is awareness aware of itself. Whether those objects are emotional or mental or physical, always there is awareness aware of itself.

Pure vigilance must be an ease of recognition; otherwise, there is *doing* vigilance, and this is already not vigilant. When you hear this thought, *Now I am going to do vigilance,* ask

Rest in vigilance and see. Just wait and see. See what the destiny of the body is. See what the momentum of the lifetime is. There will be objects passing by the altar of vigilance. Let them pass like clouds. Clouds are no problem, certainly no problem from the sky's point of view. You are the sky. You are not an entity looking up at the sky. You are the sky looking at the appearance of entity.

yourself, *"Who" is doing vigilance?* This is direct self-inquiry. You will see that there is no one there, there is only vigilance. And then you will see that it is quite natural to be aware of passing objects as well as aware of what is aware of both passing objects and itself.

It is a mistaken understanding that implies vigilance to be a burden. The real burden is the denial of your beingness as awareness itself. The idea that vigilance is a burden comes from the *concept* of spiritual practice. You are admonished to practice. You have to keep your practice. I don't know what the word *practice* is translated from, but it is a bad translation, because in English practice means some kind of preparation for a real event. You practice for the football game. You practice for your recital. You cannot practice for life. Life is right now. So I don't use the word *practice* in terms of vigilance. I am talking about *being* vigilance. Be that now. You are that already. Recognize yourself as that, and be vigilant to your true nature. Then see. Without looking for anything, see.

In Western culture, particularly in America, we are trained to know what is going to be ahead and to attempt to make it be what we want it to be. This is why there is so much suffering here, trying to force life to be something based on a particular concept. Then we search for agreement with that concept and fight any disagreement of that concept. Even if we are victorious in our fight, we are left unsatisfied, unfulfilled.

Wait and see doesn't necessarily mean you sit on your couch and never move. It also doesn't necessarily mean that you get off your couch and move. It is much deeper than that. An active life can be lived as vigilance, and an inactive life can be lived as vigilance.

There will be many insights. There will be many revelations and deepening experiences. In the midst of it all, be vigilant to what has not moved, what has always been whole, what has always been radiant and unpolluted. There will be even deeper insights. Enjoy them as they come, wave them good-bye as they pass, and be vigilant to what has not moved, what has not been lost by the experience of loss, and what has not been augmented by the experience of gain.

Be vigilance. The deepest joy of the human experience is to be vigilant. It is not a task. It is bliss itself. A bliss that is awake and vigilant to what never moves, to what is always present. Be that. Then you will see that this entity called *your lifetime* unfolds exquisitely, as a flower unfolds. As it begins to die, it will die exquisitely, as a flower dies. You don't need to dip it in wax so that it will stay forever at a certain stage. Death is not the enemy. Fear of death is the enemy. Fear of death is the result of the misidentification of yourself as some particular entity. Your true identification is the sky of being.

vigilance: a call to deeper surrender

the story
of "me"

When you look at an individual infant and follow that infant through the stages of individual growth, you can see that the difference between the infant and the six-year-old is quite remarkable, as is the difference between six and sixteen, sixteen and thirty-five, thirty-five and eighty. You can start to see a certain pattern of accumulation.

Obviously, an infant is born with certain genetic predispositions, tendencies, and personality, but in general the infant is open and fresh. That is why we love infants. Openness is lovable. Even when babies are difficult, they are mostly lovable because of their fresh, open, inquisitive, free gaze at life. As the infant matures, there is an influx of form and sense perception, which is put together according to the evolutionary process of the individual and that of the species. With the sixteen-year-old, the momentum has already shifted from openness toward personal accumulation and gain. The struggle of adolescence is a breaking free from infancy and naiveté into independence, knowledge, and power.

Even in the most wonderful lives, usually a burden is being carried. This burden is born out of identification with the so-called personal accumulations. This life burden, or individual burden, is *the story*.

A story has to be magnetized by a point of view. That point of view is the mysterious identification of oneself as a particular individual. Let us call it the generic *me*. It is the magnet that attracts sensations and experiences and then translates them into story—your life story. That story is the dream. It is possible to wake up in this dream.

I love a good story. There is nothing wrong with a good story. A good story can be profound and beautiful and entertaining, both in its sublimity and in its horror. A good story usually has complexity, mystery, success, and failure; and a true story has resolution at the end, bringing it all together.

In certain individuals, at a certain point in life, there is a recognition that the story is not wanted. At least the part of the story that is not liked, that weighs heavily and keeps one identified as something less than what is yearned for. There can be many attempts to see the personal, individual story in a better light, perhaps it even can be seen from the perspective of truth. This is glorious and wonderful, for in a better life, the identification of oneself as *victim* falls away, and recognition of oneself as *hero* or *heroine* or even, possibly, *enlightened one* arises.

the story of "me"

Most of you reading this are in a special position. Relative to what the burden of your life as a six-year-old or sixteen-year-old was, you are either in heaven, or you have at least glimpsed the heavenly state. You have at least visited it, and you recognize, *This is where I want to live. Heaven. Because in this promised land, I am the welcomed one. I am anointed and glorified and worshipped and recognized as God's own child.* This is a beautiful story, and I would not take that story away from anyone, except for the purposes of our investigation. True investigation reveals what is beyond both heaven and hell. My teacher asked that I bring this opportunity of investigation to you.

To hear that, to really hear that, you must accept the invitation to drop the whole story and ask yourself, *If it is all made up, if "me" does not exist, then what is real? Who am I? What is true?*

What perpetuates the story of *me?* Desire fuels the story. Even though there may be a desire

I am asking you to investigate what your current story is. If there is still aggression or victim-hood or hero-hood; anybody doing anything to you, for you, or even with you; any scenario of escape, attainment, gain, loss, or position; recognize it as a point of view, and tell the truth about it. This story can be subtle, and in its subtlety, it has the most power. The most subtle story is called *subconscious*. In your willingness to tell the truth, you see what story is being told over and over based on a particular individual called *me*.

The story has many flavors and colors and sensations, and it is exquisite in its own right. But it is not true. *Me* does not exist. *Me* has been made up for at least as many years as the particular body that is identified as *mine* has existed on this planet. It is totally and completely and arbitrarily *made up.*

to let the story go, a desire to see what is true, there is also a desire to continue making up the story. This must be recognized. The desire to continue the story, whether that desire be seen or unseen, is rooted in the fear of being nothing. The fear is supported by the belief that if you let go of this story that has been told so diligently throughout this lifetime, you will be nothing, you will die. It will be the end of *you*.

If you look carefully, you will see the subtle yet powerful conscious effort to keep *me-ness* in place. Maybe now it's an enlightened *me*, but it is still *me*. The fear is that without some conscious effort, maybe the body will just disintegrate on the spot. The fear is that if the body disappears, *who you are* will also disappear.

To whatever degree that there is fear, that is the degree that there is misidentification with the story of you as the truth of who you are. To the degree that there is identification with the story of you as the *truth* of you, there is suffering because you are not a story. The story is a lie, and a lie is a burden. It is a burden that is maintained every morning, every day, and every night. Maybe at night the burden is put aside for a while so that there can be deep rest, but it is picked up again as the body leaves the sleeping state. It is augmented, decorated, rearranged, fixed, balanced, and made better—made into a better burden. There is nothing wrong with that. If you are going to be entertained by a story, then yes, balance it, make it right, decorate it. But usually what happens is that the story becomes an object of worship in the name of either self-hatred or narcissism. Then this story of *me* is the burden of suffering.

I am not speaking of *nothing* as the mind hears nothing, as some kind of nihilistic, flat, dead void. Pure *no-thing-ness* is conscious intelligence. The infant doesn't know its name and so doesn't relate to itself as a name but relates to itself as conscious intelligence. The story of

The first challenge is to recognize that you are telling a story. Then the challenge is in having the willingness to stop telling the story. The willingness to die, and in that, the willingness to be nothing at all. Then this that we have called *Self* or *Truth* or *God* is revealed to be that very same no-thing at all. You recognize yourself as that no-thing.

infant, adolescent, and mature human is the story of the emergence of *me,* the worship of *me,* the burden of *me,* and the release of *me.* End of story. Back to conscious intelligence. Consciously knowing oneself to be the conscious intelligence in which all *me's* make their appearance and disappearance.

Many individuals have awakened to the truth that individual consciousness is inseparable from universal consciousness. Often whatever is left of the momentum of the apparent individual consciousness has gone into hermitage or isolation from society. At a time in the absorption of the apparent individual consciousness of Ramana into the pure consciousness of universal being, Ramana had to be fed. There was no interest in keeping his body alive. My teacher, Sri H.W.L. Poonjaji (Papaji), made a bridge between the life of the sadhu, a life story removed from the interactions of society, and the life of the active person. Papaji lived outside the sheltered ashram. He had a family; he had a job; he had day-to-day interactions with other persons who had no inkling of self as consciousness, all the while knowing himself to be the totality of it all.

I don't know what is the destiny for your life. Whether you live your life as a hermit or whether you live your life in the middle of the marketplace, you have the full potential to recognize the truth of your inherent no-thing-ness.

survival, sex, and personal power

As the shift occurs from the projecting power of mind to the resting power of mind, there is an awareness that in order to perpetuate the story of *me*, there have to be three major story lines or thrusts. At the shift point you can begin to recognize more clearly the obsession and fixation on these three major lines. All threads of the story are rooted in survival. The initial and foundational story line has to do with survival of the body, with all the gross and subtle ramifications of that primary thrust. From that foundation, all other story lines have to do with either sex and/or power.

These threads are maintained by retelling your story innumerable times even in a single day. They are initially set up for very good reasons. Identification of self as individual body supports survival of body. If the baby doesn't cry, the baby most likely dies. There is the need for sex to have more babies. There is the concern with one's position in the herd so that the body is protected (even exalted) in service to survival.

At this time, at this stage in your life, you can recognize that these threads have to do with the story of *me-ness* and the perpetuation of the body—*me* equaling body. Now there can be the deeper recognition that certain thoughts don't actually need to be thought any longer. That, in fact, the capacity to handle hunger is already in place, and there is no need to think, plan, or obsess about hunger.

In this moment you have the opportunity to stop the unnecessary continuation of the story so that the subconscious following of the story can become conscious. When it is conscious, there is a choice to stop the obsessing, to stop the addiction, to stop projecting the story, to stop rehashing the story, and to trust that all the appropriate survival mechanisms are in place.

The same is true with sex. Perpetuation of the species is no longer an issue. Sexual energy may appear, but the perceived need to obsess about it only causes unnecessary suffering.

The obsession with personal power, elbowing into the herd so that there is protection, or elbowing up to the top for extra power, brings the same suffering.

Right now you have the capacity in your life to recognize that this lifestream, through whatever blessings and luck, has food and shelter, has leisure time, and has the support to actually consider what is deeper and even more meaningful than survival, procreation, and power. This is a rare and most precious treasure. Throughout our history, and in the world situation today, most people don't have this opportunity. But for you, in the midst of plenty, survival is not the issue. Of course, you can make it the issue. You can concern yourself with better and better survival, with more and more guarantees of survival, but if you tell the truth, survival is really not an issue for you. You have to make it an issue. You have to perpetuate the striving, the elbowing, the crying, the suffering, the demanding of guarantees. That perpetuation is the practice of telling the story over and over and over—past, present, and future—evaluating, checking, weighing, and fixating.

You have a very privileged life. You can always find those who are more privileged, but mostly you will find those who are less privileged. What will you make of this privilege? What will you make of your ancestors' struggling and fighting and demanding so that you could have this privileged life? How will your time be spent? How will this particular lifestream be spent? Where will your attention be?

No one can answer this for you. There are great saints and sages and awakened beings who call you to a deeper life, whatever your circumstances. Most of you have tasted every form of

You know how to get food. You know how to get shelter. You know how to get sex. You know how to get personal power. And you know that if your attention is fixated on that, you can never get enough. There will never be enough. If your attention is freed from that, then what you have is always more than enough. What you are is always more than enough.

sensual pleasure. Where is your attention now? Is it in retasting and retasting? Or is it freed for a deeper, unknown exploration?

When I speak of freedom, I am speaking of freeing attention, allowing attention to freely explore, and to not obsessively attend to what has been taken care of long ago. That war has been fought and blessedly won. Now what will you make of this peace time?

Most people will generate another war. It gets the juices flowing. It is something to do—an enemy to fight, allies to gather. The real challenge is to be peaceful, to be who you are, to honor what has somehow been given you in this lifetime. To honor that is to share it. Then your lifetime becomes peace recognizing peace everywhere, regardless of circumstances.

the most ruthless
act of a lifetime

The sacred books and the great teachers have often said that the awakened being is very rare. This has been true in the past. Whether it is true in the present and in the future is up to you. This takes a resolve that is so total it is immeasurable. When resolve is total, then resolve is absolutely easy.

I often have occasion to read the most exquisite letters of opening and deep realization. They have inspired you, and they have inspired me. But finally these letters mean nothing. They mean nothing when the writer of even the deepest letters falls for phenomenal temptation. The letters reflect truth, they display truth, but your life as you live it now *is* the reflection of what you really want. If what you really want is truth, then you will live in surrender to that and not in surrender to phenomenal display. Whether it is the phenomenon of personal power or sexual excitement or spiritual power, it is all a trap of the mind.

When phenomena that have been cast aside appear in another way, through another door, promising more glory, more beauty, more thrills, the usual pattern is to slip back into the pleasure trance with the thought, *Oh, yes. I've waited for this forever. I'll get back to truth later.* Haven't you taken truth for granted this way?

From the first satsang, I have said over and over that this resolve is not casual. It is not trivial. This resolve is the most extraordinary, the most rare, the most unusual possibility of a lifetime. In embracing and surrendering to this most

If you surrender to the truth that no phenomenon can ever touch, you are free. Your life is then a beacon of freedom. This is a freedom having nothing to do with comfort or discomfort, likes or dislikes, excitement or dullness. It is true freedom. The truth of who you are *is* this freedom, and these phenomenal displays are simply masks, clothes, passing clouds, chemical/electrical moments.

extraordinary opportunity, you have the support of every awakened being, in all the realms, throughout time, before time, and after time. Still, it is totally up to you. You are supported, you are cheered, you are shaken, you are cajoled, and still it is *up to you*.

True surrender is the most ruthless act of a lifetime. It is the willingness to die to all hope of pleasure—*all* pleasure. Then see what is received. You cannot surrender to truth so that you will get more pleasure. You have tried to make that deal, and what you have gotten is more suffering. Even with extreme pleasure, there is more suffering.

You must expect the deepest, vastest, most thrilling displays of phenomenal temptation. You must expect to arise what you have hungered for in the most secret recesses of your mind. Whether it is some display of personal power, or an appearance of the hungered for soulmate, or

Resolve is not a trivial matter, but what makes resolve difficult is the attempt to hold on to some idea of personal gratification. Ironically, this in itself is hell. When you are willing to fully face whatever temptation, horrible or exquisite, and to die to all fantasies of personal gratification, you discover gratification itself as who you are.

the winning of wealth or personal recognition, whatever lies in wait will present itself.

This is the invitation that is spoken in satsang. This is the message from Ramana and Papaji. You can expect to be pushed and pulled and flipped, to be attacked from the side and the back, to be presented with flowers and sweets, to be clubbed. This is called Leela, the play of consciousness. Leela plays very hard. If you are surrendered to truth, then this play will only push your mind deeper into truth. If you are, in fact, surrendered to some phenomenal experience, your mind will be pulled out of the experience of your own being as gratification itself and back into the search for *more* or *different* or *better*— the names of the gateways of hell.

investigating the nature of phenomena

It seems I've been given a very active mind, and the phenomenon of personal success is very big right now. My new work has just been released, and I'm receiving a lot of praise and attention.

If you investigate turning the active mind's attention to itself, what is discovered? Praise and adoration come and go, as hate and attack come and go. If you put your attention on the current of bliss that is within you, this current of bliss will reveal a river of bliss. This river of bliss will flow naturally into an ocean of bliss. This ocean of bliss lifts up into a sky of bliss. The sky of eternal Self is truth. If life presents roses or if it presents ashes, the sky of eternal Self is the truth. You may like the roses and hate the ashes, but attention to truth reveals stillness beyond likes and dislikes.

Then isn't truth to be found in phenomena as well? Aren't they one and the same?

You cannot say that until you have realized phenomena are nothing. Otherwise, you are using a spiritual concept to justify the following of phenomena and wondering why you keep suffering. Forget that! *One* is too many. *The same* is ridiculous. It doesn't even make sense. See what is immovable.

Using spiritual truth to serve egoic understanding is a trick of the mind, and I see it in the most tragic ways. Forget any concept of *all is one,* because if you are remembering it, you are using it as some justification for following phenomena, and this is the trap.

When you attend to truth, you are acknowledging what no phenomenon has ever touched— the truth of yourself. Not hating phenomena, and not loving phenomena; just attending to truth. Truth is permanent. Phenomena are impermanent. You know this essential distinction from your day-to-day experience. This is not esoteric. It is very concrete. Things come and go. Thoughts come and go. Emotions come and go. People's responses come and go.

Your attitude about yourself comes and goes. Good, bad, up, down, excited, flat—all of that comes and goes. Truth remains present, alive, available, blissful. Attend to truth, and phenomena are simply comings and goings. Not only are they simply comings and goings, but they are actually vehicles for deeper realization of truth.

This is a ruthless, unsentimental cut. The desire for this cut is why people traditionally retreat from the world of phenomena and live the life of a sadhu or a recluse or a monk. But the world of phenomena that must be left is the world within your own mind. Retreat from your interpretations, your measurements, your qualifications for at least one instant, and in that retreat, see what is available. Then you have the opportunity for true, free choice, for true intention. Then you can truly ask yourself, *What is it I want?*

I can guarantee you that many people want phenomena, and they will spend however many lifetimes chasing more things, more experiences. If what you want is Truth, then take one instant to let go of everything you thought would give you Truth, and experience what is already here. Then and only then do you have choice. Either you will say, "I simply, absolutely choose Truth," or you will say, "I choose the phenomena."

Forget everything, and in that instant you will see what is permanent. Attend to that. Surrender the mind to that. Then the mind cannot be busy. The busy-ness is in attending to phenomena. In a quiet mind, the deepest realization naturally occurs because it is already here. In your attendance to phenomena, you overlook what you already have, which is what, in fact, you hope phenomena will give you.

The whole process seems to be just surrendering to what is.

If you are surrendering to phenomena and calling phenomena *just what is,* then you have played a nasty trick on yourself. Phenomena are what come and go in what is. In order to surrender to what is, you must first discover what is. Do you understand? What *is*, is truth—permanent, eternal, unchanging presence.

This kind of misunderstanding is common: *Hey, I'm just going with what is.* We have tried all of that in the name of freedom, in the name of Truth, in the name of choice, but it is really in the name of *I've gotta be me.* That is not what *is*. What *is*, is unchanging. All phenomena do arise from that, are never separate from that, and do return to that. But in this deep disease of conditioned existence, there has been attention paid only to phenomena, and this brings unnecessary suffering.

It is possible to stop unnecessary suffering, but it is not a casual stopping. It is stopping attending to *me,* and recognizing the truth of *Is.* Only when truth is realized are phenomena no problem.

If for one instant you surrender to *is*-ness instead of surrendering to phenomena, then you honestly have a choice. It doesn't mean you are any less *is*-ness if you choose to follow your mind. Maybe you like to suffer. Maybe you like drama more than peace. That is all right at certain stages, but you are here in satsang to discover the possibility of choosing truth—permanent, eternal, never-going-anywhere truth.

what is being protected?

People often ask me how to surrender, how to be still, because surrendering and being still are really the same. There is no *how* to surrendering or to being still. The *how* is in how the mind holds on, how the mind resists. That's a very important how, because when you discover how the mind holds on, and how that holding is being defended, then surrender simply is ceasing to hold. The insight into why it is being defended will come naturally. You don't have to go looking for the whys. They will be revealed.

The challenge is to tell yourself the truth. What is being defended? What is being protected? Then there can be choice. There is nothing wrong with protecting and defending. It doesn't mean you are not the Self. It doesn't mean you won't go to heaven. It doesn't mean you won't succeed in nondual realization. It doesn't mean anything. That's the joy of it. But the activity and focus and attention on how to protect gives a false meaning to what is being protected.

I am not speaking of the body. The body needs protection. While the body is here, protect it as well as you can. Clothe it, feed it, shelter it. When the body is sick, rest it and give it medicines. What I am speaking of is something much closer than the body. Something that has an imaginary wall of protection and defense built around it. The tragedy of that wall is that it is only a defense against your Self and the realization of your Self.

Inquiring what the mind is protecting is really the same inquiry as *who* is protecting. I've noticed that in questioning *who*, there is often a jump into nondual understanding, a jump over the wall of defense, and then ten minutes later, an hour later, a day later, a month later, there is the experience of suffering. I would like for the function of the wall to be addressed. What is this wall protecting?

You don't have to tear down the wall. You don't even have to see that the wall is an illusion, and what it is protecting is an illusion, and the protector itself is an illusion. That is all true, but in this moment, tell the relative truth about what is being protected, what is being defended. This is the activity of mind, the strategizing and planning, the getting something or keeping away something else. At the root of these strategies of mind is some form of defense, some form of protection.

For this moment, let's forget that the protector is unreal, even though it is absolutely, totally unreal. Let's forget that the wall is unreal, even though it is absolutely, completely unreal. Let us see what is thought to be protected, because in that seeing there is the capacity for the mind to let go, to be unprotected, to be still. To be still is to be *un,* period.

the weather theory of emotions

When it comes to the emotions, we still live in superstitious times. We imagine ourselves to be sophisticated and realistic, relegating superstitions to another era, to a time when people would see a solar eclipse and, thinking that God had left them, would cry out, "What have we done? What do we need to do to get the darkness to move off the sun?" Then after people performed rituals, sure enough, the darkness would move off the sun, and there would be great rejoicing and release. Those rituals would then have to be performed over and over to keep the darkness from coming back. When the darkness eventually did come back, new rituals would have to be devised.

It is easy to see the superstitions of the past, but we are often blind to the superstitious practices of today. One of those superstitious practices is the relationship we have with our emotions. Often they are clung to as if they were signs from God—signs of either anointment or of being sent from the Garden. This superstitious relationship is the cause of many kinds of suffering.

For example, fear may arise, perhaps as part of the genetic makeup which is based on survival. Because we are psychologically sophisticated and have read many books telling us that if there is fear, then there cannot be love, there is great concern around the fear. A huge amount of time and energy is then spent in the attempt to get rid of fear. This is superstitious behavior. We want to be free of the so-called negative emotions, so

When anger or fear or despair arises, there is the opportunity to simply stop, to not do anything in relationship to it, to not act it out, to not deny it, but simply be still *as it*. Then a wonderful discovery is revealed.

we have constructed sophisticated psychological and meditative techniques, different escape hatches, for dealing with them. These are all built around the superstition that these emotions actually, inherently mean something, rather than seeing them as simply weather. A storm comes, it is most unpleasant, some things get battered, some things get ruined, but the storm passes.

The sun itself is never eclipsed. If you are standing away from the sun, and a cloud passes in front of the sun or even the moon, it appears as if the sun is eclipsed, but from the sun's viewpoint, the light continues to shine.

What if emotions were stripped of their meaning and significance? Then where is one's whole identity as it has been known? Perhaps the subculture that you find yourself identified with takes emotions as evidence of depth. Relative to numbness, emotional experience does have more depth, but in our arrogance we assume that one's emotions and passions are the deepest truth of oneself. When these passions are acted out, indulged, or identified with, they are really just distractions from the true passion, the call into the depths where there is no you.

I am not recommending that you not feel emotions. I recommend experiencing them all the way to the core. And when I say experience, I do not mean acting them out. Expressing emotions has its place, but here we are speaking of direct, complete experience, and it is rare for superstitious people to directly and completely experience powerful phenomena.

Maybe one of our ancestors simply experienced the eclipse of the sun without doing anything. What a relief! Then this person could shout to the rest of the human family, "It doesn't mean that much. Really! It passes on its own."

When you discover that these emotions, these sensate phenomena, do not in reality exist as you have thought them to exist, when you discover this thought or phenomenon called *me*

In the willingness to experience totally any emotional phenomenon, whether it is anger or happiness, fear or courage, you will discover, in truth, that it does not even exist. In the willingness to experience totally who you think yourself to be, you will discover that who you think yourself to be, in truth, does not exist. It is only assumed to exist, and that assumption is held together by sensations, and conclusions about those sensations, which keeps one on the periphery, in the shallows, rather than diving into the depth of experience.

does not in reality exist as you have thought it to exist, then you discover what does exist, what *is* existence. What a discovery this is! Then whatever appearance a phenomenon takes, it is recognized to be nothing and does not need to be fought or denied or indulged.

the skillful use
of emotions

When I last saw you, I said that I wanted to burn up. Since then I have had several experiences of burning. A couple of nights ago I woke up in the middle of the night, and for the first time in my life I felt real fear. At first I got mentally involved with it and I thought, Okay, where did this come from? Is it from another lifetime? *How do I explain this? Finally, I let myself just be with the terror, and it just kept coming and coming. Gradually, I had a sense of falling through it. I was just there and it was moving through.*

And this morning, what is the experience?

That fear can come and can go, and there is a part of me that is separate from fear.

What is that part?

It is what is here when fear is present and here when fear is not present.

So there is a part that is independent of fear, that exists whether fear exists or not?

Yes.

When fear arises, does this fear exist independently of that part?

No. The fear is part of what is observing and experiencing it.

So the fear is part a of totality, and yet the whole is whole, with or without fear?

Yes.

I speak a lot about the skillful use of emotions because emotions do appear, strongly in many cases, and we are a particularly emotional culture. Since there is no real necessity to spend all of one's energy on sustenance for the body, there is an enormous amount of energy that then

Excellent. There is a very useful Buddhist term, *skillful means*. Skillful means here means the right use of emotion. The skillful use of fear is to meet it consciously, undefended. Then fear naturally reveals what is whole, what remains when that which passes has passed. These are natural insights. They are not learned, they are not theoretical, but are directly discovered.

searches for someplace to fixate itself. In our culture, the tendency is to fixate on the emotions. We want to get rid of certain emotions and keep others. This desire/aversion response leads to building mental barricades. These barricades in turn give rise to suffering.

We have a particular superstition that fear and terror can't be met, so we spend enormous amounts of energy trying to construct a barricade against it. Yet in the middle of the night, or in some unforeseen circumstance, we see how fragile that barricade is.

I am happy to hear this report of consciously meeting whatever the mind has attempted to protect oneself from. This meeting reveals stillness—stillness meeting stillness. The revelation, the insight, the realization that arises from this meeting is what all spiritual endeavor throughout time is pointing to.

Skillful means is the capacity to recognize this well of terror and to not move from that recognition, to consciously meet it. This is what you are reporting. To consciously meet whatever appears fully and completely is awakening, because meeting anything fully and completely reveals Self, reveals what *is*. Fully meeting all reveals that whatever is being met is something passing through that which is meeting everything, that which is permanent.

boundless
love

My struggle has to do with feeling that I don't know how to live, I just exist.

This is not the problem. The problem is thinking that you do know how to live and then struggling to make life match that thought. I read a wonderful quote recently: "You know how to make God laugh? Tell Him your plans!" Yes, it is a good joke. The problem is imagining that life can be known, that there is a *how to* manual you can follow.

You are born and you exist and have a life. If your life is made totally different by becoming ill and you find yourself in a body that's foreign and uncomfortable, then you start your inner struggle to be who you are all over again.

Who?

I got lost.

Yes. What you are describing is the lost-ness. First, you imagined yourself to be the body that got born and is subject to disease and suffering, as all bodies are. That's the nature of birth and death. Then you got lost in your identification of yourself as some body that got born. The truth of who you are has never been born, is not even subject to birth. It is what gives rise to birth, what is before birth. That is who you are. In that realization, you are found, and in that finding you will shout out, "I was never lost! I only imagined myself to be lost in a body, struggling to figure it out."

You are here in satsang. However you imagine yourself to be, you are here. Imagine yourself as a body, you are here. Imagine yourself as God, you are here. Imagine yourself worthless, superior, nothing at all, you are still here. My suggestion is that you stop all imagining here.

There can be no confusion unless you are trying to find yourself in your thoughts. You cannot find yourself there. Sometimes your thoughts are good, and sometimes they are bad. Sometimes they are open thoughts, and sometimes they are closed. You are before all thought. Simply return attention to what is before all thought. You don't have to go anywhere for this return because that which is before all thought has never been born and is not subject to coming and going, appearing and disappearing. It is before thought, during thought, and after thought. Eternity itself is before confusion, in the midst of confusion, and after confusion.

Are you saying it just is?

Yes. I am saying *you are*. Before this body, after this body, and during this body—*you are*. Now, if you understand only intellectually, then

At some point in your life a maturity arises where you cease imagining you can find yourself in any mental understanding or in any thought. Then regardless of thoughts, in whatever confusion arises, you will not be looking to your thoughts for release. This moment is now. *Now* does not mean in the present. Now is before past, present, and future.

the next satsang you go to, you will say, *I am,* but still there will be no release. I am not speaking of a mental understanding. I am speaking of realization. Realization does not come through searching for it in thought. There is some idea that if you just think the right thought such as, *I am God,* or *I am free,* or *I am enlightened,* or *I am realized,* or *I am That,* then everything will be solved. But these statements come *after* the realization. Do you understand that?

I think so. Am I confused because I'm trying to heal myself with my thoughts?

Yes, you are trying to heal what is already whole. This is very confusing.

I've been told by doctors that I can heal myself, and now I'm hoping and thinking that maybe I can.

Yes, but when you refer to yourself, you are still talking about your body. The body, ultimately, cannot be healed. You can heal one thing but eventually something else will fail. Eventually, all bodies end.

Okay. What I'm trying to say is that the blockage is not the body, it's the pain.

No, it's not even pain. It is some relationship with pain. It is the thought, *No, I don't want pain.* This *No, I don't want pain* arises because of identification with your body as who you are. You imagine that experiences through the sensory system have something to do with who you are, that they can tear or puncture or pierce or fragment who you are. That is called *conditioned existence,* and you are trying to heal that, to put Humpty Dumpty back together again.

Every time I try to do anything to change the energy, I'm constantly faced with chaos and blocks and tests and more struggle.

What if, right now, you don't make any attempt to change anything?

Where is the problem then?

Well, today is the first time in four years I've been able to sit comfortably on the floor and meditate, and in doing so I realized that when I'd get warm and start to cough, and I thought I was sabotaging my meditation, I would just open up and a breeze would come through the door.

But you are still speaking of the body. The body is subject to comfort and discomfort. The body is subject to fragmentation, to being pierced and punctured. The body is subject to death. That is not what I'm pointing to. I am pointing to who *you* are as that which cannot be punctured because it is not a *thing*, that which cannot be fragmented because nothing can be separate from it. As long as you identify yourself with this body, there will be suffering. There will be pleasure and there will also be suffering. For a moment, stop trying to change anything. Stop trying to keep, stop trying to keep away. Do you see?

The body will rot. You know that. Some bodies start earlier than other bodies. You observe this in plants and other animals. Some plants and animals are very healthy and vital and some are not. That is just the nature of form. Who you are is not subject to rot.

You glimpsed it in that moment, and there was peace.

I am not saying don't take care of your body. I am saying that you cannot truly take care of your body until you realize that taking care of your body has nothing to do with who you are. First wake up to who you are, and then whether you take care of the body or don't take care of the body is secondary. Until you wake up, you will confuse taking care of the body with finding happiness.

The body gets in my way because I like to stay focused and balanced, and the body's pain seems to interfere with that, and I get chaos. . . .

This is only more of your confusion. This is all just some idea. Let everything go. Don't try to change anything. Don't try to keep anything. Don't reject anything. What's the big deal then?

Fear.

Fear! Where? Where is it?

Tell the truth now. In that moment when you turned to find the fear, in the very instant when you turned to look at it, what did you discover? Don't lie to me or I'll throw something at you.

(laughing) You're making more fear!

I don't see any fear. In the instant when you looked, there was no fear. There was nothing. You met it with investigation, with inquiry, in innocence. To get it back, you had to make it up again. You thought, *It can't be so simple; it can't be so easy.* Well, it is.

Yes.

Now be still. Be open. Stop telling yourself a story of what needs to be and what needs not to be—*If only that were fixed, then this would be fixed.* This kind of mental activity is an addiction. It's a mental sickness, and it simply distracts you from what is always whole and healthy. *You are that which is always whole and healthy.*

When you recognize that, then yes, take care of the body. Take care of the Earth. Take care of your brothers and sisters, your parents, your lovers, your children. But first realize who you are; otherwise, this *taking care of* is still an attempt to extract health and wholeness from some mental image. It is no good. It doesn't work. Certainly, now you have realized it doesn't work. It's the work of the devil, of Lucifer. The devil is the tyranny of the mind.

Do you know the story of Lucifer? Lucifer leaves the right hand of God and descends into his own kingdom where he can be the ruler, where he can say what is and what is not. That is called *Hell*. When Lucifer returns to the right hand of God to finally lie in prostration as the servant of God, then Lucifer is true to his name, Angel of Light. When the mind recognizes it is only a servant of God, then the mind is useful.

when nothing
is something

I recently had a conversation with someone who has been going through a period of suffering. A number of times throughout our meeting this person said, "But I know it's nothing. I understand that it's nothing." That's the truth, it is nothing, but it was apparent that this person hadn't truly realized that. As a way of avoiding that discovery directly, there was instead his mantra: *I know it's nothing, it doesn't matter, it's really nothing, nothing's really going on.* This is the danger—taking the truth and filtering it through the mind until it becomes another defense mechanism. It is to be expected, so be alert to this danger. Saying that suffering is nothing, or even remembering an experience of it being revealed as nothing, is all useless. Assume that it is something. Assume that it is real, and then see, what is it?

All of these strategies have their place in the development of the individual consciousness. Things can happen to an immature mind that are too big for the being to handle, and so coping strategies are devised. There is nothing wrong with that. These strategies are appropriate in certain times and places. But at some point in the maturing of a particular individual, the desire to know the truth arises. The desire to see clearly reveals the futility of all the strategizing. Maturity reveals that suffering cannot be escaped by indulging, covering, denying, acting out, or blaming. It is recognized that the suffering avoided through strategizing only grows larger because there are more thoughts, more stories, and more

The usual way of dealing with
discomfort, from mild to extreme,
is to attempt to hide from it or to
escape. That escape takes many
forms. You know these forms well.
Ususally, there is blaming. You blame
your faults or others' faults or the
world's faults. There is justification.
You make excuses for indulging the
suffering and negativity. You give
the excuse weight and prominence
and importance. There is denial
of suffering. You act as if nothing
is going on, going into a kind of
dissociated trance, walking around
like a stone saying, "Nothing's
going on."

emotions that are factored into it. At that time there can be disillusion regarding the capacity to escape. This disillusionment is the beginning of the potential for the mind to open and discover that suffering can be met fully and directly. If suffering appears again, the challenge is to meet it with no idea of what was revealed in the last meeting. To meet suffering with an open mind is to consciously suffer. To consciously suffer is to be freed from the reaction to escape. When you are freed from the command to escape, you can realize what suffering really, finally is.

In a true meeting, an explosion of love and clarity and truth occurs. The essence of oneself is revealed, teacher to student, friend to friend, lover to lover, parent to child, mind to suffering. If you begin to imagine what the next meeting will give you, the true meeting is lost, is now the property of the past, and the bondage of avoidance of suffering begins to take root again. At first it may be subtle, and then as it is fertilized by either denial, justification, blame, or conceptualizing its nothingness, suffering becomes more gross.

This is the edge. As long as there is a body functioning and existing in this apparent world, there is mind. There cannot be a body without a mind. That mind can be a peaceful, open, sattvic, welcoming, investigating mind, or it can be a closed, dissociated, blaming, strategizing mind. The opportunity in this lifetime is to tell the truth about what is going on in the mind.

The vigilance required is a ruthless willingness to tell the truth about identification, to tell the truth about whatever story is going on in the mind. If there are strong, continuing emotions, you have to recognize that there is some story going on, even if you aren't aware of the content. Maybe it is subverbal. Maybe it is not consciously coming through, but there is still some story of suffering and some story of a sufferer. In the willingness to tell the truth, you have the

With any teaching you must be aware of the tendency for the mind to take that teaching and make it into another strategy, another excuse, or another attempt to escape. There is nothing wrong with that. It is not that the mind is wrong or bad. It is just the nature of the mind. In fact, it is very useful. It is humbling. It is the antidote to any notion of arrogance or superiority or reaching some *place* where you cannot be touched.

When you are willing to feel and to say, "I am touched by this; this hurts; what is it?" then you will see what cannot be touched, but not before. If it is before, then it's a trick of the mind, and what a master trickster this mind is. If you like a rough game, then it's a delight. Obviously, you do like a rough game.

opportunity to meet either the suffering or the sufferer. Both meetings are self-inquiry. Both reveal the nonexistence of suffering and the nonexistence of the sufferer. But this is revealed only in a true meeting, not in a concept. The concept is simply a support for the belief in a sufferer saying there is no belief in the sufferer! To say that there is nothing going on is actually in support of something growing bigger.

There is no problem with emotion. Emotion is part of the texture of life. Anger, fear, grief, and sadness are all just passing weather. But the continuation of a particular emotion through time indicates some story is being made up by the mind, with subtle or not so subtle thoughts, and then thoughts upon those thoughts.

This is the trickiest challenge. It is a spiritual challenge. Before this, the challenges are simply to get through the day, to hold it together, to find the escape. This is another level of challenge, and it is not to find the escape, not to hold it all together, not to keep it pat and safe. This challenge is nothing less than the invitation to true vigilance.

seeking the
quiet mind

I have been watching you on video, and there has been much clarity and revelation. I've had days where I've felt very centered, and the mind has been quiet. In the past I have done a lot of meditation, and there is this idea in my mind that truth or enlightenment means having a quiet mind. And now meditation just doesn't seem to work for me anymore. When I sit down to meditate, and I ask myself, Who is meditating? *it just doesn't happen.*

What doesn't happen?

It's just not satisfying. I've done Transcendental Meditation and other different techniques, and I've seen that meditation is still something of the mind.

I understand the word meditation to mean *no-mind*. The moment of meditation is the moment when no-mind is recognized to be at the core of all appearance of mind.

I have those moments of recognition periodically throughout the day, but usually when I'm having a thought, I'm just lost in it.

Are you? Or is this thought, *I'm lost in my thoughts,* just another thought that's being believed. We assume that thoughts have validity, but check and see. Are you lost in your thoughts?

Not in this moment. But when I go back in my other life, the mind just keeps chattering away, and I feel like the mind should be quiet.

The thought to shut up?

Yes, the thought that the mind should be quiet. The thought, *The mind should be quiet . . . but, why isn't the mind quiet?* The authority of

Isn't this thought, *I feel like the mind should be quiet,* the noisiest thought of all? But this particular thought is somehow believed to be valid, as if it's a *super* thought.

that thought is believed, and believing that authority is a disruption of the quiet. Silence is naturally present. It is not a matter that it *should* be here.

When you think, *I'm lost in my thoughts, and I shouldn't be,* just stop for a minute and question that assumption. To directly question that assumption, ask yourself, *Who is lost?*

Yes. When all of this mind chatter is going on, I ask myself, Who is listening to this stuff?

And what do you find?

Nobody.

And in that moment, where is the mind chatter?

In that moment, nowhere. But then that moment is gone, and the mind chatter keeps coming back.

That's right. Thoughts keep coming back because they have been fed lifetime after lifetime. Not even just your lifetime, but your ancestors',

Thought is a beautiful power. It is not the enemy. Thought is just thought. It is a product of the imagination, and it can be exquisite. It can be a beautiful veiling of reality or a horrible veiling of reality. But when thought is investigated, it is discovered not to be separate from consciousness itself. Thought is consciousness at play with itself. But in this play, consciousness somehow thinks itself lost, and that thought generates other thoughts about how to find itself—what is needed, what was done wrong. Each layer of thought gets tighter and tighter and more and more entangled.

your neighbors', and all the collective lifetimes of thoughts being fed with more thoughts.

The thoughts feel like something coming together and squeezing.

Okay, so it feels like that. But when you investigate thought, what is it?

It's the same as emptiness.

That's right. This is obvious. It is not esoteric. It is not because you've done a hundred thousand prostrations or because you have been practicing meditation or not practicing meditation. It is simply that when the nature of thought is directly investigated, the mind's attention is turned toward itself, toward self-inquiry, rather than turned outward, building thoughts upon thoughts.

Who is really here? What is really here? What is really going on? Nothing can survive this investigation except no *thing* at all.

Does it ever get to a point where silence is more apparent than thoughts?

Who cares? In this moment, you tell me, who is it that cares?

I don't know.

When you actually turn your attention toward silence, is there any more measuring? Is there any more checking to see, *Am I there yet?*

Not right now. But it's very easy in your presence.

That's what this relationship is all about. It's about realizing the ease of self-inquiry, this gift that comes from Ramana and Papaji. Experience the effortlessness of it, the absolute ease, and seize this opportunity to stop worshipping and practicing your belief in thoughts. It is not about making thoughts wrong. It is not about blanking out. It is finally to simply see that thought is thought, and what is not thought, what cannot be thought, is who you are.

effortless realization

I was reading Ramana, and he said that efforts toward self-realization could only be made in the waking state. The question that came to mind was, Who is making the efforts?

That's a very good question.

It can't be the ego, because why would the ego participate in annihilating itself?

Ramana said that effort only relates to the ego.

[At this time, the wooden stool the questioner is sitting on suddenly and inexplicably breaks and gives way.]

Whoa! Talk about the ground being pulled out from under you. Wow! So, then the question . . .

Oh, let's just rest for a moment in the beauty of that! The support of the apparent questioner just let go!

Okay . . . so has the Self forgotten itself?

The Self has *appeared* to forget itself.

Why has it appeared to forget itself?

So that it can appear to remember itself.

Then it's just a game, right?

Yes! Because in the instant of real self-remembering, can you say it has ever been forgotten?

No.

That's right.

So it's true what I read in Ramana's book that there's nothing to realize? Finally, the final truth makes sense. There is no creation nor destruction. There is no mind nor body nor world. There is no bondage nor anyone that is bound. There is no liberation nor anyone trying to attain that state.

What's the problem then?

A doubt comes into my mind that says, Is that it? Just that?

If the realization that you just spoke is followed by, *Is that it?* then it has not been realized. Maybe it is understood in a certain way, and there is a memory of an experience that makes the words valid, but the realization itself is *huge*. It is not diminished in any way. Realizing everything to be essentially nonexistent is not a diminishment. The ultimate diminishment is not a diminishment!

So all the big inner experiences happen through grace, and there's really nothing the ego can do to further that?

The truth is that the ego doesn't do anything anyway. The ego is a thought, like a garment. It's not the garment that does anything. The ego is inanimate.

It's an impostor.

The mind searches for a place
to identify, for a place to grasp,
and it sorts through everything
based on past experience. You are
reading Ramana's book of truth,
maybe for the third time or the
hundredth time, and now because
of some other experiences the
words are coming together
in a certain way.

But if your conclusion is, *Is that it?*
put the book aside. Put every word
aside of Ramana or Gangaji or
whomever. Let the whole ground
open, nothing to hold on to, no
ledge, no ignorance, no liberation,
no-body. Let them all go. God, soul,
everything that you have clung to
throughout time has gotten you to
this point. Now fall through
the point.

Yes, but not an impostor as an entity. It's an impostor as a mask, as a persona, as a veil, or a sweater. Stop misidentifying the Self with its garment. There can be some residue of the appearance of life in the ego, as when you take off a sweater that you've worn for a very long time, it may even appear to stand on its own! And you may think, *Oh no, it's coming to get me!* But if you examine it, you realize, *Oh, it's not really alive. It's my sweater, a garment. It just has the residue of my life in it.*

When I get frustrated, it makes me feel better to remember the realization that it's all just a game. Is it really just a question of forgetting and remembering?

No, it's a deeper question. The most sacred memory can serve as a beacon, a sign. But the truth is, even in letting go of that memory, even in not referencing any moment to any other moment, however sacred, there is the revelation of what is permanent, of what is not located in some experience in some time, but is here now. That which is permanent wears all clothes and discards all clothes. It appears to remember, and it appears to forget. It appears to be reborn, and it appears to die.

So even the sacred experiences I've had can be a trap in the game?

I wanted to say one more thing. Someone once said to me, "If you're attracted to Gangaji, that means you're ready to give up the search." What I thought was, Okay, my search will end with following Gangaji forever and forever. *And what I got today was that the search actually stops Here. It stops Here. I stop my search. I don't go any further, Here.*

That's right. Then you are not following Gangaji. You are following what stopped Gangaji. That is the true teaching, and it is nothing Gangaji can teach. Papaji said to me, and I see it more and more as true, that the true teaching leaves no tracks at all.

Yes, even the most profound experiences, when remembered, can be a trap. I am not saying to dismiss them or to trivialize them. Just recognize the potential for those experiences to become objects, and in that objectification, there is once again the overlooking of the ever-present subject which gave rise to the experience, which is present before and after the experience, which cannot be forgotten, and in truth cannot be remembered because it cannot be congealed into a concept of memory.

What do you mean, "What stopped Gangaji"?
That which stops you.
Now I'm afraid.

You're afraid because you still perceive yourself as separate from that which stops everything—that which is the immovable presence of being.

I said that to Papaji. I said, "Oh, I'm afraid." And he laughed and said, "It's only because you imagine yourself as separate from all of consciousness. When you know that you are consciousness, and everything is contained within you, there will be no fear."

it's time to
tell the truth

Over the years of traveling around and speaking with people, I have seen that there is clearly a deep, strong, and true desire to *wake up*, whatever that means to any particular individual. There is a true desire to realize God, to realize truth, to stop the violence, to stop the hatred, to stop the suffering, and to wake up to what is possible in this lifetime. If you want to awaken one hundred percent, if that has priority over everything else, then immediately you are awake. That's the truth. I stake my life on it. My life is a guarantee that if you want to awaken to your true nature,

The biggest obstacle to awakening I've seen so far is that awakening is actually wanted for something else. Awakening is wanted for feeling better, or so that you don't have to be the same person you think you are now, or to get some recognition, or to forget all the bad things that you have done or that have been done to you. Awakening is wanted as a vehicle or a tool, and there is frustration that this tool is not given to you. This doesn't work.

Truth must be desired for itself, regardless of any consequences that might follow. This is a shocking truth. We are so used to wanting something to make our personal lives better, and God knows, we have tried. Luckily, most of us have become deeply disillusioned with the possibility of getting rescued, of getting something else that will fulfill this true desire to awaken.

if you want that totally, you will awaken to your true nature.

I am asking you to look inside, to be ruthlessly, relentlessly honest and truthful with yourself, to see why you want to awaken. What will awakening give you? If your answer is something beautiful or grandiose or altruistic, such as peace on Earth or harmony among all people, put that aside for just a moment and see if truth, this unknown state of awakening, is desired for itself, regardless of consequences. I am asking you to tell the truth. We spend most of our lives lying in both gross and subtle ways. The lying gets very intricate, and the web gets tighter, and you know this.

There is an opportunity now, in this moment, to discover what it is you want for its own sake, without getting any comfort from it, without it taking care of anything. I can feel the fear that this evokes. This is not a usual consideration.

You are an adult. It is time to tell the truth. I am asking you to tell me what it is you want truly for its own sake, and if you still imagine somehow you don't have that, let me know what you imagine keeps you from it. Let's examine it and see: is that obstruction to truth real or is it part of the webbing, part of the fabric of your imagination?

It's very easy to play in the drama of awakening, saying, "Oh, I'll get it someday," or "He has it," or "She has it and I will just be in the aura of it; then I can keep my lies and my web."

the edge of
surrender

A question that often arises in satsang is, *How am I to know when the command I'm receiving is coming from Self, from Truth, and not from my ego, from my mind?* This is a legitimate question, yet there is no formula I can give you for checking. This is the ruthlessness of freedom. The possibility of mistaking Self for ego, and ego for Self, is huge and constant. It is not a game for children.

Children are given very clear instructions: "This behavior is right and that behavior is wrong." These instructions are important for children; otherwise, the children just do whatever they want, whenever they want. You know this from your own experience of being two years old, or sixteen years old, or even thirty-five years old: *If I want it, it must be right.* Then in new age or spiritual circles, this gets translated into, *It must be right because my heart says it is so.* But with some degree of experience, you discover that what can feel right, can feel good, can also cause huge suffering. Murderers often hear divine voices saying, *Kill.*

I can't say that there is no suffering related to me. There have been people who have stormed out of satsang, who have felt assaulted, who have felt that they were not being honored. I am not happy that they felt assaulted or didn't feel honored. But to make them feel honored, I would have had to tell a lie about the truth of who they are. In satsang there is a command that I have been given to tell the truth regardless of consequences. Even though lying may be more comfortable at times, I cannot perpetuate the illusion

All religions will give you formulas, and you can go by those and cause no harm, cause no suffering. You can live a life that is relatively peaceful and harmless, and still it is not a free life. So the question is, is it possible to be free and cause no harm, cause no suffering?

of bondage, even bondage to the most sublime, elevated, and necessary codes of behavior.

I understand what a dangerous statement this is because I know the workings of egoic identification. I know how easily truth can be twisted into some justification for following egoic desires and pleasures and puffed-up proclamations of transcending normal codes of behavior.

This teaching by Ramana and Papaji is radical, and one of the greatest dangers of this transmission is this very issue—the issue of how easily the mind can take a realization such as *all is one* or *nothing exists,* and make it serve the purposes of ego.

It is possible to be so ruthlessly honest that neither pleasure nor pain is the determining factor for action, so that if there is justification for re-identification and the following of egoic desires, it can be experienced and starkly seen. Then every persisting desire can be a vehicle for self-inquiry. *Who* desires? *Who* wants?

In responding truly to that question, it can be revealed that there is freedom from wants, freedom from desire, that there is no one wanting anything, and that no one is yourself. If you are willing to know yourself, you love yourself. If you are willing to love yourself, you see yourself everywhere. And what you love, you don't harm. This is the finest edge possible. There is absolutely no room on this razor's edge. There is no room for *you* on it.

In our particular age, we are still experiencing a reaction to an earlier era when there was a generalized, consensual repression so that everything could appear okay. People were nice to one another, and society did actually function well for certain groups. But the repression eventually became unbearable, and there was a huge reaction in the sixties and seventies that we as a subculture largely reflect. This reaction was built upon telling the truth, but unfortunately it wasn't the whole truth. The eighties and nineties were further refinements of repression and reaction. Now that we are interested in self-inquiry and in telling the whole truth, we see that reaction no longer works. Repression/reaction has generated a huge amount of suffering and misidentification. Perhaps it is that very repression/reaction that has given rise to the possibility of deeply asking oneself, *What is it that I want? What is it I really want? Is it just another fulfilling sexual adventure? Is it just keeping the lid on so there is no discomfort? Is it just another possibility of the promise of survival? Is it just another way of promoting myself through status and position? Is it just a way to deny myself through belief in worthlessness?* These are the areas where desire is the most subconscious. These are the areas that have kept the organism moving forward, sexually preserving itself and finding its rank in the herd. These are the issues that will give rise to the strongest impulses to listen to the mind.

You will certainly make mistakes. That is the nature of this Leela. That is the nature of there being no room for *you* on this razor's edge. The willingness to meet the mistakes and the suffering, the willingness to die to issues of survival, sexual pleasure, or social ranking reveals the possibility of recognizing what needs nothing, wants nothing, *is* nothing. It is a bonding with everything in love and compassion and empathy. It is a most ruthless task. It is the edge of vigilance and surrender, and no one can do it for you.

After Ramana awakened, he stole some money and ran away from home without letting his mother know where he was going and causing her great distress. He was not being a good son. He was not following the mores of his culture. Perhaps he should have told his mother. Maybe he made a mistake. Who can say? We don't need to either worship that act as correct or judge it as incorrect.

What was seen as correct in one generation is realized as incorrect in the next generation. Within every generation there is a huge blind spot. When you look back at slavery, you cannot help wondering how it is possible that this horror could have occurred, and it occurred with the acceptance of good people! We have to be willing to see what is occurring in our own lives, just as horrible as slavery, that we have been blind to. In the willingness to tell the truth, it is possible to see where we are denying or ignoring some aspect of our own being, and in that denial, causing great harm.

The mind searches for a formula, a code of living. The truth is that you have plenty of formulas, plenty of codes, and the absolute truth is free of it all. Freedom is free.

how will your life be used?

How is your life being used? It is obvious what the common uses of a lifetime are—accumulation of both worldly things and spiritual things, in the hopes of being saved from death—and none of it works.

You are all very familiar with your own practices of accumulation and how much of your life is used for that. Whether the practices are subtle or gross, they all come under the heading of trying to make life fit your image—either your image of who you think you are, or who you think you should be, or who you think God is, or who you think the perfect person is—and then the constant activity of letting those around you know how they don't fit this image. This is the usual, isn't it? How much time is spent looking to see how others are not conforming to what you think they should be doing or how they should be doing it?

I invite you to discover that source and to be true to it. If you have not discovered it, be true to it anyway and let it discover you. You are irresistible when you are being true, rather than just continuing to live the life that was passed on to you based on images, concepts, and ideas, or rebellion against those images, concepts, and ideas.

When I first met Papaji in India, in a very humble room, I remember being overcome with the recognition that all my prior images of *heaven* and *bliss* and *the teacher* were worthless. God was alive and the bounty of heaven was undeniable in that room with mold on the walls, with

The greatest challenge is surrender
to truth. Of course, if you have any
image of what truth is, that is not
truth. No image is separate from
truth, but truth remains independent
of any image, any concept, or
any thought. The deepest, most
profound challenge is to surrender
to what is untouched by any idea,
evaluation, or conclusion past,
present, or future. It is to discover
who you are, closer than any image
of yourself, any sense of yourself,
and deeper than any experience you
have ever had or could ever have of
yourself.

The challenge is to be true to
that, to be true to the source of all
thought, the source of all sensation,
the source of all imagination,
without understanding it, without
grasping it, and without getting it.

screeches and stench coming in from the street. It was different from my fluffy, pink, shiny Sunday school image.

It was very good for my Western mind to be stopped in that way, and I can remember the subtlety of then attempting to make myself over to fit the new image. I stopped wearing all makeup. I didn't look in mirrors. I liked the new humbleness and wanted to be finished with all Western ideals. One day Papaji looked at me and said, "Why don't you fix yourself up?" He saw so clearly how I was attempting to grasp an image of truth and to look like that. Then I saw that I had done that all my life. When a certain era would come in, I would attempt to fit into the image of that era, whether it was to look like a hippie, or to look spiritual, or to look like an intellectual, all the time knowing it was not quite that. Truth cannot be *looked like*. It is wherever you are, in whatever form. It wears no

Truth cannot be *looked like*. It is wherever you are, in whatever form. It wears no lipstick and it wears bright red lipstick. It wears no clothes and it is clothed in golden robes.

lipstick and it wears bright red lipstick. It wears no clothes and it is clothed in golden robes.

The attempt to model truth is continual entrapment by the mind, which knows only images, concepts, and ideas. When we speak of freedom, we are speaking of what is inherently free from any image, concept, or idea. That is who you are. However you have imagined yourself in the past, whatever you hope you will become in the future, this is who you are already. You can immediately discover this by discovering what has never been touched by any of it. It is alive within you right now. There is nothing you have to do to get it. Since it is who you are, you are in this moment fully capable of realizing that. All that is required is to give up every notion of who you are for one instant.

How easy just to drop every idea! You have to continually maintain these ideas, and you have done this for so long you don't even notice the energy you put into, *I am a human being;*

I am male; I am female; I am good; I am bad; I am inferior; I am superior; I'm getting it; I'm not getting it; I had it; I lost it; I will get it; they got it . . . and on and on. This is a lot of activity. This is the common use of a lifetime. What is unusual, what is offered to you by your own self, is to wake up to who you are, and to let this lifetime be used by that awakening, with no idea of how or when or what.

This is what I have come to say to you. This is what I will continue saying to you until this body drops. You have the opportunity to listen, to investigate, to discover for yourself, and to choose.

When I met Papaji, I felt myself to be quite neurotic. I had enormous images and concepts, and I was constantly evaluating myself as either living up to those images or not living up to them. Papaji stopped me in my tracks, and he sent me to stop you in your tracks. The rest is up to you. Since you are freedom itself, since you are the Self, you have the freedom to let this lifetime be used as you choose. Maybe prior to our meeting you didn't have that freedom, I don't know. Maybe no one had ever told you you were free. Maybe you believed all kinds of ideas about destiny or free will or no free will. In our meeting, you have a second chance. You can investigate it to see if it is true or not. You may have thrown away the first twenty, thirty, fifty, sixty, or eighty years of your life, but now you have a second chance. It is up to you. This is precious time, this whole lifetime. It is a lifetime where you can at least hear the call of freedom. What a precious lifetime! How will this preciousness be used?

about the author

Born in Texas in 1942, Gangaji grew up in Mississippi. After graduating from the University of Mississippi in 1964, she married and had a daughter. In 1972, she moved to San Francisco, where she began exploring deeper levels of her being. Today, Gangaji offers Sri Ramana Maharshi and Sri Poonjaji's radical invitation to stop the search for fulfillment and enlightenment and to fully recognize the truth of one's being, which is already completely whole and permanently at peace. She lives in Ashland, Oregon. Visit her at *ww.gangaji.org*.

hampton roads publishing company

. . . for the evolving human spirit

Hampton Roads Publishing Company publishes books on a variety of subjects, including spirituality, health, and other related topics.

For a copy of our latest trade catalog, call (978) 465-0504 or visit our distributor's website at *www.redwheelweiser.com*. You can also sign up for our newsletter and special offers by going to *www.redwheelweiser.com/newsletter/*.